The Prayer of Jabez In The Marketplace

10 Days To Enlarge Your Business In The Marketplace

by

Deborah Franklin

The Prayer of Jabez In The Marketplace

by **Deborah Franklin**

i

Dedication

This book is dedicated to all the business owners who want to have their territory enlarged. To all the family and friends who are praying for you and to the persons who invested in my dreams to help them become a reality. I'm so grateful for their trust and belief in me. My prayer for them and all the persons that are reading this book, is that God will continue to bless you and enlarge your territory.

Table of Contents

Introduction

This book was birthed out of the need to see my business grow and find its purpose. I was looking around me and seeing so many people going places and doing things that I was not doing. I was just going to my job and as we say just making it work. Then I heard God say do not get comfortable where you are, and I was not in the right place.

I began to pray God I know there is more for me and I know you have not destined me to work for someone all my life. I knew that I had a gift and calling but not using it to my fullest potential. Then God brought back to my remembrance the Prayer of Jabez. I started to study it and meditate on it. God gave me so many revelations that it just blew my mind. God said do a 10-Day Challenge, I was like who me??? Cannot be me. I do not do this, that's for other people.

I had to be obedient and not only do it but do it online. This had to be the scariest thing for me. I've done online things before, but never a challenge like this. Whewwww, I was scared. But when I began to hear the testimony of the people who had completed the challenge with me. It confirmed that I had truly heard from God. Now when I saw my territory begin to enlarge, I was walking in total amazement. You know that feeling when you have been praying for something and it comes to pass that is that feeling I had.

To be honest I was shocked and amazed to see how God was moving on my behalf. Now wait for it.....God told me to do the challenge again. I was like huh.... God said, "Do it again, but this time its going to be to be a book and journal" In my mind I was like stop playing with me.

I listened and did the challenge again and I tell you God gave me new revelations and I saw the boundaries of my territory enlarging by leaps and bounds. This challenge was also developed to work with the 'The Prayer of Jabez in The Marketplace Journal'

Day 1-Alignment

The Prayer of Jabez 10-Day Challenge is going to be phenomenal! Day 1, being intentional and personal.

So, who is Deborah Franklin? Deborah Franklin is an author, a speaker, a media coach, a preacher, and a teacher. The reason why this is important for me to say now is that I know that I am changing with what I'm doing and how I'm doing it because for a long time, I never wanted to merge my "my personal, business and faith" together. And God started to show me that I was tripping. So, know that this is a major step for me to even share that piece of information with you.

OK. So why is this challenge important? And I know some of you might be thinking, "Yeah, it is and all that." Because in this challenge, we are going to gain clarity, initiate your purpose, and initiate your destiny. And some may say "I already know what my destiny is. I already know what my purpose is." I already know and I think I'm clear. But you know what? You might think you know what this is, but you may not know for certain.

The Prayer of Jabez In the Market Place

So, during this challenge, over the course of this next 10 days, I promise you, this is either going to be a time that God is going to confirm what you are thinking, or He is going to expand what you are thinking. He is going to confirm and expand. And I promise you all, you are going to understand this because I went through this and it totally blew my socks off.

When I did this challenge myself, I'm not telling you my whole life has changed. I'm not sharing this with you because I didn't do this myself. I'm not sharing this with you because I just jumped up one day, "Hey, let's go ahead and do the Prayer of Jabez Challenge." No. I experienced this, and I just want to share some things with you about that so you can gain the clarity like I did. So you can get the clarity of where you're going and why you're going through that, and then that's going to help you understand why it took me on this journey of discovery of who I was as a person, who I was as a minister, who I was as a business owner, who I was as an educator, and bottom line just who I was.

And so, when you get that clarity and you can initiate your purpose and identify your destiny, you are going to be – oh my god! You are going to see so many things open up for you that you are just going to be like, "OK, God, I got this. I'm ready. Now, just come on."

All right, y'all. So, let's jump on in here and we are going to look at the Prayer of Jabez. The Prayer of Jabez is found in 1 Chronicles 4:9-10, "Jabez was more honorable than his brothers. His mother had named him Jabez, saying, 'I gave birth to him in pain.' So Jabez cried out to the God of Israel, 'Oh, that you would bless me and enlarge my territory! Let your hand be with me and keep me from harm so that I will be free from pain.'

Jabez is praying about enlarging his territory. But, most of all he is being specific about what he wanted. He is making an alignment of here he is going and what he is doing. So, when you think about alignment, a lot of times, we talk about alignment, but we don't really know what the word means.

But let us look at it like this. OK, I am a words person. I must look them up. When we look at the word alignment, it is a noun. What is a noun? It's a person, place, thing, or idea. So, alignment is an idea. An alignment is something that you must do within your mind. You must do this in your thought process.

So, it says, arrangement in a straight line or in a correct or appropriate relative position. Usually when we think of alignment, we think about putting blocks together. We think about putting certain situations together. We think about lining up, making an alignment with who our bosses are, making an alignment with who our friends are, making an alignment in our relationships, making alignment in building. So yes, that is true.

But it also means that it is a position of agreement or alliance. So that means that you must be in alignment with everything that you do regardless. Again, back to your job, your relationships, and people that you hang out with, and we wonder why they are off kilter because we are not in alignment. You have got to start lining yourself up with people that are on the same wavelength so you can start advancing to the next level. That is why they say some friends and situations are seasonal. Some people are for your now, some people are for later, some people are put in your life to be with you the whole time.

And then you begin to wonder relationships, and I'm not just talking about personal relationships, I'm talking about any type of relationship that doesn't last or doesn't work, it's because your alignment is off.

And now, when we are looking at the Prayer of Jabez, we need to get our alignment with God lined up because we want certain things to happen. And that's why when you are praying this prayer of Jabez for these 10 days, we are going to be so intentional, so personal that we are getting ready to take our lives to the next level because we are going to be intentional while we are working on our alignment to God to set us into the right direction. So, you have to start thinking, "I have to be in alignment."

Now, let us get ready to take it another step further. If we are putting things in alignment, that means we must make it personal. So, when we look at the Prayer of Jabez, the first line, I want you to put your name, so right here I will put, "Deborah Franklin, cried out to the God of Israel, 'Oh, that you would bless me and enlarge my territory! Let your hand be with me and keep me from harm so that I will be free from pain.' And God granted me."

You see how I made that personal, me, my request. Or if you want to put that personal pronoun there, I put my personal pronoun. I feel like I should put "me" there. But if you want to put "her" there instead of "him" or if you are a man, you could leave it as "him" but if you are a woman of course, you can put "her."

And then like me, I wanted to take it a step further. I didn't want it to be a pronoun. I want it to be me, so granted me my request. Because when you put it as me, you are saying, you are believing right then that He is going to do it for you, that it may not have happened, see, that's activating your faith because when you activate your faith, you are believing that God is going to grant you what you are praying for.

You believe that God is going to take you to that next level because you made it personal and you activated your faith and you activated what you needed — what you need to activate is your mindset to change because so many times we pray about things but when we pray, but we doubt. And in order to make this thing work, we have got to pray, have faith, and believe that it is going to happen. So again, we are making it personal.

All right. So, we made it personal. Now, let's make it intentional. Yes, I said that. We are getting ready to make it intentional. So, in that first line, you are going to put your name. But then where you see enlarge, what do you want God to enlarge for you? Is it your business? Is it your family? Is it your thought process? Is it — what is it that you want God to enlarge for you? And you want to put that on that line.

So, "Deborah Franklin cried out to the God of Israel, 'Oh, that you would bless me and enlarge my business, my coaching business, my media coaching business, my publishing company, my podcast. Let your hand be with me and keep me from harm so that I will be free from pain.' And God granted me my request."

You see how I made that personal? Put in that thing what you are praying for and being intentional about. Put in there what you are being intentional about so then you know you are being intentional about what you are asking God for, because if you say, "Oh, God, just increase my business," what business? You may have 5 or 6 different businesses, or you might work with somebody else's business.

But you have to be intentional with what you are praying and asking God for so then when it starts to come to pass, it makes it measurable. It makes it – it makes you be able to identify and then we are being – you are being intentional. You are being laser-focused on what you want God to bless you with in this season.

All right, we are making it intentional. We are making it personal. Now, I know you weren't expecting this on day one. You probably weren't expecting me to get as intense as I am with you but yes, you have some homework. Yes, you do! You got some homework! And get ready. Get ready. Get ready. Get ready. Get ready. Because we are not going to go through this10 days and not have any evidence of what we are doing.

All right. Put your prayer in several areas so you can pray it continually. So, in other words, write your prayer down. If you got to put it in the bathroom or on the mirror, if you have to put it in your car, on your rearview mirror, on your dashboard, in your cubicle, again, it's, wherever – in the kitchen, it doesn't matter. You got to put it wherever you go. You want to be able to pray this prayer continually. All right? You see what I'm saying? Put your prayer in several areas so you can pray continually for it.

Then you are going to activate your faith that is going to happen. In other words, you are going to start believing. So again, in it says – the Bible also says, "Faith without works is dead." So, when you have faith, you are putting in the work. You are praying your prayer. You are looking for ways to make – for God to enlarge your territory.

You are believing God to start dropping things into your mind and into your spirit that you are going to be able to activate. You are waiting and you are intentional about what you want. You know in your heart of hearts that God is getting ready to bless you beyond whatever you could ask, think, dream, or imagine. You are setting yourself up for God to expand you. You are accepting and this is going to activate your faith.

Then activate your faith that is going to happen for someone else. In this season, we cannot pray just for ourselves. We are going to activate our intentionality because I believe if it can happen for me, it can happen for you, and that all things work together for the good of them that love the Lord. And it works together for the good of them that seek His face. It works together for the good of them that aren't selfish, that take everything that they need and be able to move on with it. And God is getting ready to do a miraculous thing. And I just believe in my heart that He is getting ready to move like never before and He is getting ready to activate so many things for us.

Complete your homework for Day 1. I want to see what you have to say because we are going to be believing God with you and for you that it will happen, that it will come to pass, that God is getting ready to enlarge your territory like never before, that God is getting ready to do things in your life and around your life like never before, that you are getting ready

---

to be where you want to be because you have sought God's face and God is taking you to another level.

Day 2 Pain

Prayer of Jabez Day #2. Now, I told you from Day 1, this challenge is going to be extremely interactive. This challenge is going to push you, it's going to help you go to the next level, it's going to help you get ready for the doors that are getting ready to open for you because we are going to eliminate those distractions, those things that are hindering you, and that is why we are doing this challenge. That is why we are working together. That is why we are taking things to the next step.

We are going to go into the deep parts of your mind and the deep parts of your thought process, in those deep, dark areas that you have not talked about because in 2020, we cannot go into this thing not doing what we are supposed to do and being distracted by those things. Because when we are distracted then we have problems. When we are distracted, we can't go to the next level. We can't do anything that we want to do because we are operating in the realm of distraction. We do not want to operate in that realm.

The Prayer of Jabez In the Market Place

So, let's go ahead. Get started. Welcome again to Day 2. I know you are excited like I am. I just cannot wait. This challenge so far has been, oh my gosh, been a blessing to me and I do pray that it has been a blessing for you. And this is Day 2.

All right. Let's go ahead and recap. We say, "Why is this challenge important?" This challenge is important because #1, we are going to gain clarity, and #2, we are going to initiate our purpose, and #3, we are going to identify our destiny. For some of you, you are going to initiate and or you are going to activate. For some of you, need to identify.

All right. So that is why this challenge is important. We are taking this another step further. We are looking at things a little differently.

All right. So, let's go ahead and open with our Prayer of Jabez. And it is found in 1 Chronicles 4:9-10 and it states, "Jabez was more honorable than his brothers. His mother had named him Jabez, saying, 'I gave birth to him in pain.'"

Wow! I had named him saying, "I gave birth to him in pain." So today we are going to be dealing with pain.

"So Jabez cried out to the God of Israel, 'Oh, that you would bless me and enlarge my territory! Let your hand be

---

The Prayer of Jabez In the Market Place

with me and keep me from harm so that I will be free from pain.' And God granted him his request."

All right, guys. So, we talked about being intentional, how you are going to make it personal. Remember, every day we are going to build on something different.

Now, I said when I first started reading the prayer that his name means pain. His mom gave him this name because he caused her pain. And I was like, wow! All kids caused pain from what I've been told when they are birthed.

And so, when you think about it that way, did he cause her more pain than the other ones? Because he was still more honorable, she treated him. And you know he lived through that name. And so, I started thinking, what does pain mean, remember I told you, we are going to be looking at what words mean. Pain, it's a noun as well. It's physical suffering or discomfort caused by illness or injury.

Then the second part says careful effort, great care, or trouble. That means that you really – you work hard to cause this pain. You really work hard. So, we want to look at the pain because you know, he even says in the prayer that he didn't want to cause any pain. So now, we have made it personal. We have made it intentional. And then now, we are going to make it even more intentional. We are going to take our prayer to another level.

All right. So, we see what we filled in the blanks. You are filling your name then it says what you want to enlarge. And now, you want to be free from pain that you would not cause any pain, but what has caused you pain. And you do not want to cause pain that somebody caused to you. So now, we are going to put in there what has caused us pain and then declare we are free from that pain.

So just like I told you before, I'm going to make this intentional. So, the prayer would go, "Deborah Franklin cried out to the God of Israel, 'Oh, that you would bless me and enlarge my business, my speaking business, my coaching business, my publishing company business, my preaching ministry. And let your hand be with me and keep me from harm so I will be free from the pain that was caused for me from past relationships, the pain from someone talking about me behind my back and stabbing me in my back, the pain of growing up and people would call me names and basically bullying me and I had to suffer from verbal abuse.'"

Yeah, we are getting real deep right here. Some of you have not even thought about the pain that someone that you needed to be free from. And then it states, "And God granted me my request."

You have not thought about that pain. You are wondering why you cannot move on. It is because you are still being locked down by the pain that was caused to you by someone or an entity. So yes, I'm talking about truth hurts. Yes, I'm talking about someone at your job. Yes, I'm talking about being looked over on for a promotion. So you got to think about everybody always wants to talk about the truth hurts but nobody really wants to talk about that hurt that you felt or that pain that you felt from a job, from some type of entity, or the place that you love so much that closed, it hurts you. That is really, real. And people are dealing with that but then you wonder why you cannot move forward is because you have not dealt with it in a real personal and intentional way.

So, for us to move forth and be able to do this in this Prayer of Jabez, we again have got to make it more intentional. Make this prayer personal to you and your situation so that way you can go forth and then increase your level of expectation.

You have got to take this to another thought process. You have got to start thinking about what has truly caused you

---

The Prayer of Jabez In the Market Place

17

pain. Have you really dealt with it? Have you really thought about what is taking you out and what is making you fall into those bouts of depression? What is making you fall into those bouts of doubt? Those things are causing you pain and you need to be free from them.

Homework: Determine what is your pain? Some of you really need to think close about that. You really need to focus in on that. You really need to decide what is your pain? I'm going to let that sink in a little bit. Because some of you are saying your pain is one thing when in all actuality, it is something else. What is your pain? All right.

Number 2, next step. Seek God on how to relieve your pain.

This next step is an activity that I tell you works. And it is the first step of getting rid of your pain, getting rid of that trauma that is causing you so much pain and that is causing you to feel like you are paralyzed. That is causing you not to be able to mobilize your thoughts, your dreams, and where you want to go. That thing that makes you doubt everything, that thing that makes you self-sabotaged yourself.

Things are going well, you are happy, but you are always looking around the corner waiting for something to fail, waiting for someone to leave you, waiting for someone to lie on you, waiting for someone to stab you in the back.

Yeah. You need to really seek God on how to relieve your pain. But today I'm going to give you one more thing, one more thing to help you on that journey of relieving your pain. Whatever caused you pain, the person or the entity, write a letter to that person or entity, dead or alive. I don't care. You are going to write a letter to them. Then you are going to burn it. This symbolizes letting it go. Yeah, letting it go.

You are going to have to let go of this situation. Now, even though you have let it go, even though that this exercise symbolizes letting things go, let's just say that is your first step, you still are going to have seek God on how to really – to be able to let it go and pray for the comfort of God in helping you change your mindset. Because in order to take it to the next level, in order to be who God has truly called you to be, you have got to learn how to operate in that situation. You have got to learn how to take what you are doing and move to the next level. You have got to learn how to alleviate what is going on.

I know that Day 2 is probably not what you expected. I know that Day 2 is not giving you what you expected because Day 2 is causing you to do some self-reflection. Day 2 is causing you to have to think what has caused you pain. Day 2 is going to make you really do the work. Day 2 is like none other.

When I tell you working through these steps, they seem simple, they seem like it's easy, it may even seem like you are going to be battling like you're going to be in this fight, and actually you are. You are going to be in the fight of your life doing this, during these 10 days.

During these 10 days, you are going to start seeing things clearer. But today, during this challenge, you are going to have to get to your core. You are going to have to pull back all of those layers that you have put on, that you have called protection, that you have called closing your mind, that you have called this to be your protection when in all actuality, you are hindering yourself. This is what is causing those blocks of fear, those blocks of doubts.

I love you and I know that you can do this. I know you are set for greatness. I know that you are getting ready to walk in your divine purpose. But until you alleviate that pain, God

---

cannot enlarge your territory. Because think about it, bigger territory, bigger challenges. And do you really want to take that pain, your past pain, something that happened 10, 20, 5, 6, 2 days ago into your new territory? No, ma'am, not sir. That's like putting new wine and old wine skins. It does not work. And you do not want to get stuck in that area.

Today is all about you. I want you to take this time to really, really concentrate on what you are doing. I want you to concentrate and really start to pray and seek God on how things are going to work out for you.

Day 3 Why

Prayer of Jabez 10-Day Challenge, Day 3. Can you believe it is Day 3? We have put in some work. And I want to commend you. We are getting ready to do the work.

All right. So, let's go ahead and pray our prayer of Jabez found in 1 Chronicles 4:9-10, "Jabez was more honorable than his brothers. His mother had named him Jabez, saying, 'I gave birth to him in pain.' So, the prayer is Jabez cried out to the God of Israel, 'Oh, that you would bless me and enlarge my territory! Let your hand be with me and keep me from harm so that I will be free from pain.' And God granted him his request."

So, the process that we are going to be doing, if you have not picked up on it yet, we will always pray the Prayer of Jabez then you will pray your Prayer of Jabez when you are making it intentional and personal. And remember on Day2 we inputted what the pain was that we were getting rid of, what we had to go ahead and do our homework about last night.

The Prayer of Jabez In the Market Place

So, Deborah Franklin cried out to the God of Israel, "Oh that you would bless me and enlarge my media coaching business, my publishing business, my family, my being in ministry. Let your hand be with me and keep me from harm so that I will be free from everyone or everything that has stabbed me in the back, talked about me, used me, and deceived me." And God granted me, granted Deborah, my request.

All right. So, you see how you must make it personal and intentional, and you are going to make sure that you are praying your prayer. That is our process, guys. We will pray the Prayer of Jabez then you will pray your prayer that you have written yourself to make it intentional and personal.

Our keyword today is Why. We are going to be determining what is our why. We are praying for God to enlarge our territories. We are praying to God to take away the pain but then while He is doing that, what is your why? How many of you are questioning your why? You think you know what it is. You might not or you're not sure or you need to know how to implement it even more because guys, that is what we are going to be dealing with in this chapter.

And so, to define why, there are three definitions. And you know, it kind of messed me up because I told you, I like words, this particular word can be a noun, a conjunction, and an interjection.

A noun, person, place, thing, or idea.

A conjunction that connects, think, "Conjunction junction, what's your function?" Those of you that are in that age group, you know you heard that song before.

So – and then it can be an interjection. You know you heard that also in School House Rock. And we are going to get to that.

So, as a noun, it means that it's a reason. It's a cause, a bubbling idea, an enigma. So, remember, that is something that goes on in your mind.

So then as a conjunction, it's the cause, reason, or purpose for which or for which an account which happens. So yes, you're, like what's going on? It means it's connecting something together like, "Why are you going down the street again? And who is that and why?" So that's what you are looking at.

All right. Then as an interjection, used to express mild surprise, hesitation, approval, disapproval, or impatience, like express a mild surprise, "What?" Hesitation, "Why? Why?" And disapproval, "Just why? Just why?" And impatience, "Why?"

OK. So, you see how why can be used in so many ways to express what's going on. And I think – no, I do not think I know. Therefore we have a problem with saying what our why is because we really don't know if we are using it as a noun, a conjunction, or interjection.

So right now, when you are determining your why, it is going to be a noun because it's going to be that idea that is going on in your mind. It is going to be a conjunction because that is what is going to connect you to do what God has called you to do. It is going to be an interjection because you are going to be asking yourself all these questions because sometimes in this season, not in this season, but in this instance doing this prayer that we are doing, you are going to be asking like, "God, really why? For real? Why?" So, think about it like that in those terms when we start to develop your why.

Now, I'm getting ready to be really transparent. I am very transparent in what I do and the way that I teach. So when you look at this why, here is my why, and I'm getting ready to explain to you why these things like totally messed me up when God begin to reveal certain things to me and I had to start walking in them and then what happened when I started to walk in them. And then you are going to see how developing your why makes your personal and intentional Prayer of Jabez makes more sense.

So, for me, my why, I am a woman in ministry. I acknowledge that. I am shouting it from the mountaintops that I am a woman in ministry. God has called me in that area. I can no longer say that's for my cousins, that's for my uncles, that's for the people in my family. Now, I have to claim it for myself because as long as I was denying that portion of my why, I could not move forward.

Then I'm an author. Many of you know that I have authored three books now. Well, actually, four, and I'm getting to ready to do five. But I had not really talked about because I didn't really put it out there. But being an author is part of my why.

Now, being a speaker, that's part of my why. I speak all the time. I teach all the time. But I never claimed it. I just said, "Oh, I'm just sharing some things or I'm just doing this." But being a speaker is part of my why.

Now also, being a media coach, that is part of my why because that is something that I like to teach. I like to share with people on how they can talk on camera, how they can do teaching via webinars or through books– such as this, just like I'm doing now. I like to share with them on lighting and backgrounds and how to do certain things. That is part of my why.

And my next thing is that I'm a publisher. Yes, I am stepping into the realm of publishing. And now and look at how God is taking everything that I do, everything that I have finally admitted that I do, and He has turned it into my why. And when you go ahead and acknowledge all of everything that you do is a part of a larger umbrella of who you are and whose you are then that why is not so scary.

Now, when I was looking at these different things, I'm like, "God, for real?" Yes, this is – I know you are going to say, "But me? Why? For real?" And so, you are going to question your why. Don't question it, walk in it. Because if God has given you the vision. I have heard this and I know you have heard it too, if God has given you a vision that you can obtain easily then you know that it didn't come from God, because God is going to always give you something bigger than you ever could think, dream, or imagine because that is where your faith is activated.

See, you see how this works out together? We talked about activating your faith. We talked about activating your vision of going bigger. God is getting ready to show you some things.

Now, I know you're saying "Yes, she is crazy. She hadn't heard this from the Lord." Yes, I did. Yes, I did. And let me show you why. And let me show you how. Let me show you how I developed my why.

I want you to really look at this why prayer.

"Dear Heavenly Father, please show me my why. Let my why line up to your will and not mine so I can operate strongly in my purpose while on my road to my destiny. God, speak to me in a voice I can't deny or turn a silent ear to. I pray this prayer in Jesus name. Amen."

This prayer is so simple, so, so, so, so, so simple. And you probably said, "Why does she say that? Why did you tell me to tell God to let it be His will?" Because a lot of times, we think our why is what we think. We do not seek God to explain to us what our why, OK, and why it is our why.

And then you got to make sure that you heard it from a voice that you cannot deny, because so many times, we will hear something from God, we will hear something and we would be like, "That ain't the Lord. I know the Lord didn't tell me that." That's why I had to be clear when I pray, "God, you need to make sure that you give me something that shows me that this is You and only You."

Now for me when I know that it's not an audible thing. Usually for me, it's when things start to shut down like I heard God say, "It's time for you to move from this place," I was like, "I like it here!" But He started changing things, making things harder and harder and harder for me to be there. Then I was like, "OK, God, I need to do this."

Whenever there needs to be a shift, something always changes to get your attention. That's how I know that it's from God. Now, you know when God is truly speaking to you, it's something that you hear, it's something that you see, or it's an experience. Something happens for you to know that it is truly from God. So, I want you to pray that prayer about your why.

And again, we are calling this, The Why Prayer, your why prayer. And I want you to start praying for that and I want you to be praying that and listening

But homework, yes, you will have homework every night. Yes, we have hit this hard and heavy and I know that it has been intense for some of you because some of you had to do some real soul-searching. Some of you have really had to seek God in what you were doing.

And most of all, be honest with this whole process but honest with yourself about what we are doing and where we are going because some of you are starting out in your businesses, in your thought processes, in your ministries, or not where you think that it should be because you have not really gone through the process of letting things go from your past. You have not really started going through the process of expecting things to be good for you.

So, homework. Go ahead and fan yourself. You are probably feeling a little warm. I get it. Homework. Pray the Why Prayer. Pray the Why Prayer. And be serious when you pray the Why Prayer. So, you're going to be praying your

---

The Prayer of Jabez In the Market Place

personal and intentional prayer, The Prayer of Jabez, and you are going to be praying the Why Prayer.

It does not take long to do either one. The hardest part of this step is listening. Listen. Listen for God's answer to either confirm your why, expand your why, or change your why. Three areas. Yes, three areas. He is going to either confirm your why, He is going to expand your why, or He is going to change it all together.

Yeah, I'm going to let that sit right there. Because honestly, that's what I went through. God totally changed my why. I never in a million years would have thought that I would develop a ministry for women because that is part of my why, because I am a woman in ministry, and I have been called to minister to women.

And I never would have thought that I would have been in that position because in my mind, in my little simple thought process, I didn't think that I had experienced enough like I'm not a mother. I've never been married. I don't have — like I said, I don't have children. My career path was different. My experiences are different. So, I didn't think that I would be called to minister to women, and that's what I had to understand about my why.

Then I never would have thought that I would have reached the realm of speaking and writing and even going into the publishing realm, but it still lines up with everything that I was doing. I wanted to be in entertainment. I never wanted to be a podcaster. I never wanted to do that. I love working behind the scenes. But God said, "You are going to have to come forward because you are going to have to develop a platform for other women to be able to share their voices so other women could hear them and know that they can be a Church Girl and a CEO."

Yeah, I was messed up with that because I was like, "God, really for me? You want me to do that?" So, trust and believe, guys. Those of you that are on here with me and that are taking this journey on this 10-day Prayer of Jabez Challenge, know that I have gone through it and I am still going through it. I am still experiencing some things because God is expanding my territory. He is expanding my vision and I am going through some things that I never thought in a million years that I would go through.

You have your homework. You need to look at that homework. Because your homework is going to be key to your success in making this whole program work.

The Prayer of Jabez In the Market Place

Day 4 Message

Day 4. Can you believe it? We have been working so hard and we have been putting in so much time. I know. If you are like me, your mind is blown. God has been showing you things. You have been getting downloads and you were not even expecting things. You have been waking up, can't sleep. You have been trying to do all the things and God said, "No, do this." Yeah, I know, I know. I know. I know. I know because I am experiencing it as well.

This is not going to be a long lesson because the homework is what you must deal with. The homework is where we must start looking at because the homework is the evidence that you have been putting in the work. And I do not want you to get caught up in just saying that, "Oh, I've participated in the challenge. I did this. I did that."

But today, you are getting ready to know that we are going to share the Prayer of Jabez. We are going to be doing this challenge and this challenge is all about you. This challenge is all about you and doing what you have been called to, what you have been anointed to do and how we are going to be successful in accomplishing everything that we have set out to do. And I am really excited about where God is taking us in during this challenge and I hope that you are too.

Now, let's go ahead and read our Prayer of Jabez, "Jabez cried out to the God of Israel, 'Oh, that you would bless me and enlarge my territory! Let your hand be with me and keep me from harm so that I will be free from pain.' And God granted his request."

Now, remember, we read the Prayer of Jabez and then we make it personal. Deborah called out to God of Israel, "Oh, that you would bless me and enlarge my media business, my coaching business, my publishing business. Let your hand be with me and keep me from harm so that I will be free from the pain that was caused by other people, the verbal abuse, the not being able to get the promotion that I thought I deserved." And God granted me my request.

How have you ministered to yourself? How have you received something from that situation that you were in and then now dealing with it and being more intentional? How clear are you about that?

How are you feeling now that you have let go and have identified that pain that you were going through? You see, every day, we are going to be building on different levels, different levels, different levels, different levels.

Now today, we are getting ready to go another step further, because now that you want God to enlarge your territory, what are you going to say? What is your message? What are you doing? Have you even thought about it? Because some of you may think your message is one thing but then it is actually something else.

Now of course, you know we got to go the definitions. What is a message? A message is verbal written or recorded communication set to or left for a recipient who cannot be contacted directly.

OK. So that is like if you leave a message on the phone. Now, this is where you need to think about it, a significant point or central theme especially one that has political, social, or moral importance. This is where you are operating. You are operating in the number two. Well you are probably operating in both.

But for all intents and purposes for this lesson, I want you start thinking about what is your message? What is the

---

The Prayer of Jabez In the Market Place

message that you are supposed to be sharing not only about your business but about who you are, about your ministry? What are you supposed to be sharing in your message? What are you supposed to be sharing in your message?

Yeah, I am going to let that kind of sit there. Because some of you may have been saying, "Oh, I am a preacher that preaches every Sunday," "No, I'm just a Sunday school teacher that just wants to spread the word of God," "Oh, my business, I sell books to everybody that needs to read."

Those are good but you know what? During this challenge, God wants you to dig a little deeper. God wants you to think about where you are with the messaging that you are giving to people and for where you are trying to stretch yourself. This is the season of stretching. And trust me, I am right there with you when it comes down to it what we have to do during this entire season of stretching because I am stretching myself like never before. I am in some situations; they are not bad situations but I'm stretching because I have to go to a different level and it's time to take that leap to go to that different level.

How many of you are feeling that? Yeah, it is to come out of your comfort zone. And I know that is where I am. And for God to bless me, God has already shown me. And if you are asking God to enlarge your territory then you are truly asking God, "What is my message when my territory is enlarged or how am I preparing my message to be?"

So, let's talk about it. I can only give you what I have, what God has given me so that way you can get an idea of what your message is and what your message could be because I have really battled with this message. Trust me. I have battled. I have fought. Just like yesterday, we were talking about the why. I have been like, "Why? Why God? Why? Why? Why?" And I am like I'm really questioning – I've really questioned a lot of things that I have been experiencing. I have been questioning things that God has given me. I have been questioning like am I really ready for this? Have I really been called to this? Am I really anointed for this? Yeah, I have been questioning that.

And so that questioning is really real because I've also realized that that questioning is also a distraction. And so, we have to work on getting those distractions out and working to where we are able to share what we have and then not be ashamed of it because sometimes God gives us things that are different from everybody else. And when we are different, that causes a lot of fear. And baby, I promise you, I am right there

---

The Prayer of Jabez In the Market Place

with you. I am just going to be honest and transparent. I am operating in fear in some areas.

But I'm doing what God has called me to do and I'm never going to tell you that I'm going to get cocky in this because the minute that you get cocky, the minute you start feeling like you know it all, the minutes you stop feeling the butterflies in your stomach, you know that you are out of the will of God because you should be comfortable in doing what you are doing but you should not be so comfortable that you don't stop trusting in God to get you through the situation. And that is where I am.

When God gave me my message, I was like, "Not me. No, sir. Let me just do what I am used to doing. Let me just stay in the background." But God is like pushing me out. And so, I am going to share my message with you.

So, my message, meeting the media needs all my clients and future clients from a biblical perspective. Yeah, I've got to use the Bible to teach media. And I was like, how does that even make sense? But when God gave it to me, He is showing me some different things and some different areas because sometimes the reason why we are missing out on being able to share the word with people is because they don't feel like there's anything in there for them. They do not see that there were women in the Bible that had very good businesses. They do not realize that Lydia was there, and she had goods that the people wanted, and she funded the ministry of Jesus. She had a new testament.

We do not talk about that from that perspective. Everybody wants us to be a virtuous woman, but they are not talking about, "But then I also need some money in my pocket being virtuous." Yeah, I said it and I'm going to leave it right there.

So yes, my message that I am working on and developing is meeting the media needs of my clients and future clients from a biblical perspective.

Yeah, that is a lot. That is heavy. That is real heavy.

So, I know that you have been trying to figure out what your message is so guess what? It is the Prayer of Jabez. So, you know we got a prayer for the message. Now, if you see that this looks a little like the one that we had yesterday, it is. So, all you are going to do is I want you to write this one out. You are going to post it up again or you can start adding some comments.

The Prayer of Jabez In the Market Place

"Dear Heavenly Father, please show me my message. Let my message line up to your will and not mine so I can operate strongly in my purpose while on the road to my destiny. God speak to me in a voice I cannot deny or turn a silent ear to. I pray this prayer in Jesus name. Amen."

Yes, this prayer is simple. Yes, this prayer gets straight forward and to the point but that is about being intentional. When you are being intentional, it does not take you all night and all day to get something done. It does not take you all day and all night to share what God has given you. It does not take you all day and all night to be able to just go to God and then just sit still.

That is why these lessons aren't that long, because I want you to have the opportunity to dig in and work the process. If you set an hour aside or even if you only set 30 minutes aside to do the lesson that you take what's left after, I want you to sit still and wait to hear what God has to say about what you are doing, because I promise you, when we start going to the next days, we are growing, we are going, and we are activating different segments of what you are doing.

We are activating different segments of this Prayer of Jabez in your life because now, you are learning to pray for every step. You are learning to pray that God will fill you and anoint your mind and anoint your heart that you can hear from Him crystal clear and not be able to deny it, because you know how we are especially when we get into that question, "Like, God, for real? Like, God, for real?" So yeah. So yeah, for real.

Homework: Pray the message prayer. Then listen for God's answer to either confirm your message, expand your message, or change your message. My message was changed and expanded. Know that yours will be – you are setting yourself up for it. So, God is going to push you in a place that you did not think that you are going to be.

Yeah. Yeah. Yeah. Yeah. That is where we are. We have got to know that God is getting ready to take you to another level and I know that you are ready. I know that you are getting ready to jump out here and do the thing because God is getting ready to catapult you somewhere that you never thought that you would be. God is getting ready to send you to places. that you never thought that you would be in, send you to meetings, sitting at tables where you weren't expecting to be able to sit.

The Prayer of Jabez In the Market Place

So, get ready. Get ready. Get ready. Get ready. Get ready.

Day 5 Vision

Day 5 of the 10-Day Prayer of Jabez Challenge. We are getting to take it to another level.

Pray the Prayer of Jabez. And "Jabez called out to the God of Israel, 'Oh, that you would bless me and enlarge my territory! Let your hand be with me, and keep me from all harm so that I will be free from pain.' And God granted him his request."

All right pray your prayer of Jabez that is personal and intentional. My intentional and personal prayer. "Deborah cried out to the God of Israel, 'Oh, that you would bless and enlarge my territory of my business, of my coaching business, my publishing business, of my family. Let your hand be with me and keep me from harm so that I will be free from all the pain that was directed to me where people have lied on me, who treated me bad, who stabbed me in the back. God, let that pain be released from me.' And God granted Deborah her request."

The Prayer of Jabez In the Market Place

Yes, you can start making it even more personal, more intentional as we go on because God is going to start to reveal some things as you go through these different exercises that you are going to be doing. And I hope that you have been keeping up with your homework that you continue to pray for your message, pray for your vision, and that God just continues to bless you in this area and reveal new things.

Vision is our word of the day, have you noticed that everything that we have been praying for, they are nouns? An idea is something that is in your mind and when something is in your mind, you must develop it. When the scripture says, *Do not conform to the pattern of this world, but be transformed by the renewing of your mind. Then you will be able to test and approve what God's will is--his good, pleasing and perfect will.* Romans 12:2 NIV

A noun, the act, power of seeing, sight. Aha! The special sense by which the qualities of an object such as color, illuminates shape, and size constituting its appearance are perceived through process in which light rays entering the eyes are transformed by the retina into electrical signals that are transmitted to the brain via optic nerve.

Come on, do you see that light? The light shines in, something seen in a dream, trance, or ecstasy especially a supernatural appearance that conveys a revelation.

So that right there should have made your whole spirit jump. A thought, a concept, the object formed by the imagination. A manifestation of the senses of something immaterial, look not as visions but as realities and it is important.

The act or power of imagination, model of seeing or conceiving, the unusual discernment or foresight. Yes, Lord!

Direct mystical awareness and supernatural usually in visible form, something seen, a lovely or charming sight.

These definitions set my whole life on fire. I am ready to turn some cartwheels because you know when we start to talk about vision, we seem to leave out that vision is light. Vision must have light in order to have vision, the light must shine into the retina.

So, for you to have vision, God has got to shine on you and through you for you to see what God has planned for you.

Your vision is what has God shown you that you are supposed to be doing. Are you supposed to be feeding the homeless? Are you supposed to be taking care of someone else? Are you supposed to be walking – are you supposed to have a ministry for youth? Are you supposed to have a ministry for single women? Are you supposed to have a ministry for the elderly?

God has got to show you your vision of what you are going to operate in. And so many times we are not reaching our destiny because we are not operating with the right vision. Some of us have cataracts so that means that our vision is being clouded. Now remember, cataracts can be removed with surgery. How many of you need a vision – need a cataract removal because you have to start thinking about that because sometimes your vision could be cloudy.

But God is getting ready to show you your vision. I told you all. I have gone through this process. God has definitely been revealing some things to me and I have really been tripping because I have the vision that God has given, the message that God has given me. It is like totally blowing my mind. The vision that God has given me for this season is that to work with women in ministry and educators to help develop multiple streams of income.

This totally messed me up because I'm like, "OK God, is this why you had me go through some of the things that I've had to experience in order to be able to speak to someone where they are?" Because that is the only thing that I can think of because I started thinking about what can I do as an educator that has multiple streams of income? It does not mean that I want to come out of the classroom. But it might mean that I just don't want to work summer school or I just want to have a little extra so I can take the trip that I really want to take, and I don't have to depend on anyone

So that is what I'm talking about. Or you might just want to be saving up money with that multiple streams or like I know some teachers have taken two or three, Sabbaticals. This is the vision God showed me.

Well, what has God shown you? You already know, you got to develop your prayer for your vision.

"Dear Heavenly Father, please give me a vision. Reveal to me my vision and guide me to line up to your will and not mine so I can operate strongly in my vision and purpose ..." You see how vision and purpose must work together. "...while on my road to my destiny. God show me my vision so I cannot deny or turn a blind eye to it. I pray this prayer in Jesus name. Amen."

This is a simple prayer about vision. If you noticed, all of our prayers are going to be simple because we are being intentional, we are being purposeful, and we are going forth to God in a way that we can be able to recognize and identify what is going on.

God is going to start revealing things to you soon if He hasn't already, because I know He is revealing some things to me on what I'm doing especially when it comes down to my vision and my purpose and where I'm going and who I am and whose I am because God is doing a new thing for all of us in this time, in this season because we cannot get stuck in where we are. We have got to make sure that we are doing everything exactly the way God has intended for us to do it, because we do not want to get stuck in that place.

Homework pray your vision prayer. And then you must listen for God's answer to either confirm your vision, expand your vision, or change your vision.

Let us think about that. God can change your vision. He can change it to where things were cloudy and now, they are going to be revealed to you in all the brightness and the splendor that it should be. So, get ready, guys. Get ready for this challenge. I know this challenge is doing a lot because it is doing a lot for me and I know that this is doing so much that we have got to be ready for that.

Day 6 Discouraged

Day 6 for the Prayer of Jabez Challenge. We are rocking and rolling, and I know you're thinking I have never prayed the Prayer of Jabez like this.

But this time, I want us to look at it from a different perspective. We are making it personal, being intentional, and making it so personal that we start to heal ourselves in order to make it to that next step. We cannot go into this next season expecting the great things to happen and we have not effectively let go of everything that was holding us in our past.

All right. So, let's go ahead and pray the Prayer of Jabez. "And Jabez cried out to the God of Israel, 'Oh, that you would bless me and enlarge my territory! Let your hand be with me, and keep me from all harm so that I will be free from pain.' And God granted his request."

So now, we are going to pray our prayer that makes it personal and intentional, and by now, remember, you start out with your name, "Deborah prayed out to the God of Israel, 'Oh, that you would bless me and enlarge my speaking business, my coaching business, my publishing company. Let your hand be with me and keep me from harm so that I will be free from the pain that was caused me from people talking about me, stabbing in my back, all the verbal abuse that I had to suffer, God.' And God granted me my request."

You will think that this is kind of a weird place to put this word because at first, we were going to do something else for Day 6 but I said, "You know what? God has definitely spoken to me on this and this is where we are going to go today."

So, our word of the day is discouraged. Discouraged is a verb-is an action. That means that it is something that has had action. Not disturbed but in a discouraged kind of mode. And that means that you caused – to cause someone to lose confidence or enthusiasm.

And I am going to let you think about that. So many times, we have told people, "Don't be discouraged in this season. You got this and you are going to do this. Don't be discouraged."

But have we ever thought about what discouragement is? And because we are making this Prayer of Jabez something that is personal and something that is intentional, we want to make it be that you don't let what caused you pain discouraged you from moving to your future. Discouraged from trying new things, discouraged from trying to set out and be who you have been called to be. You start to play those head games with yourself. You start to play those games in your mind, in your heart, in your spirit where you start thinking that you're not good enough, that you're not strong enough, that you're not smart enough, that you don't have the right pedigree, that you don't have the right connections.

But all God wants you to do is just try. God wants you to just step out in faith and be like Peter.

It's OK. You can be like Peter, ask to walk on the water and just like Peter, you may sink but now you know whose name to call on for help when you feel yourself falling or when you feel discouraged. You have got to learn how not to be discouraged in this season. And sometimes it may also be a family member. It could be your children. It could be your job. Do not let those things discourage you because in this season, discouragement is more like a distraction than it is anything.

Being discouraged is a distraction, period, to get you off your game. So, what you must do in this season, in this time and for all intents and purposes of what we are doing is that you are going to make a vow. Yes, we are making a vow in this lesson. So many times, I have made a vow to the Lord but guess what? I broke it because I got distracted or rather discouraged. You can write a vow to yourself and to the Lord, but this time you cannot be discouraged or distracted. This is my vow. *I vow not to let my past hurts, disappointments, or failures to cause me to be discouraged while walking in faith that I will accomplish my dreams for my future.*

What do you vow? What is your vow going to be to yourself and to God as you prepare to embark on your next chapter? What are you getting ready to do while you are in the process of maybe starting something new or expanding your business or seeking out another degree or seeking out a new job or seeking out change? Are you going to let the discouragement get you off your path?

So, what I need you to do, take some personal time to pray and think about what is your vow going to be, which leads us to what? Homework!

Homework, you're going to develop your vow. You are going to develop your vow. Your vow is a promise to God and yourself. Like when people make vows in marriage, 'till death do us part, to love, honor, and cherish, but guess what? You are making a vow to God about you and where you are. You are making a vow to God to step out and do what you have been called to do and not let your past hurts, your past disappointments discourage you from taking that next step, and then not being afraid to speak your truth.

Again, not being afraid to speak your truth. We have got to stop operating in fear because we do not want to hurt somebody. We do not want to do this. But guess what, we cannot get free until we step out and start to speak our truth and living our true life and being – I hear these terms all the time about being authentic. Yeah, be authentic to yourself because once you are authentic to yourself then you will be authentic to other people.

I'm going to let that sink in.

Be authentic to yourself. Stop being a copy of someone else to yourself. Yes, they may have had things more than you did but only you can be you. And you need to start to be the best you that God has created you to be.

I know that some of you know that I have been on different speaking stages. I cannot be like other speakers that are out there because you know what? I must tell this. I tried. I tried to be like everybody else. I tried to speak like everybody

---

else. I tried to hide that I was a minister. I tried to hide that I had this other "life."

And I promise you, every time we went somewhere, and I spoke, the first question they would ask me was, "Are you a minister? Are you a preacher?" I'm like, "Huh?" Because you know what? Whatever is in you, that is what God is going to bring out of you. Whatever you have deep down in you, that is what God is going to use. So you have to be true to you in order to take that next step. You must be true to you.

Some of you are sitting here right now messed up because you are not true to yourself. You are not honest with yourself. Because when you are honest with yourself then you can start to fix yourself.

Yeah, I know you probably got the tears falling. I know you are probably thinking like, "How is she in my business?" Because I promise you, this is not what this lesson was supposed to be about. I was on a whole different thing, so I know God has this purpose for somebody that is reading this. This is for somebody. That you have got to pull it together and become who you are ordained to be. You have got to start to act and walk in where God has told you to be.

Yes, it may be scary. Yeah, you might be afraid. But it is time for you to step out and be free. You have got to be free because who God sets free is free indeed. And when you get set free, all the rest of the stuff means absolutely nothing.

I want you to develop your vow. And then after you develop your vow, I want you to pray your vow to God and listen for directions on how to keep your vow. Yeah, how to keep your vow.

So many times, we make vows and do not keep them. I am not talking about a New Year's resolution. I am not talking about your promise to go do whatever. I am talking about the vow between you and God and mainly that you are not going to let discouragement and distractions allow you to lose focus from your plan and your purpose.

Then after you do that, after you pray your vow and you listen for directions, I want you to post your vow. Just like you posted your prayer, I want you to post your vow. Post your vow in places to remind you of what you are working towards.

You are going to post this vow because you are going to need to remind yourself of what is going on physically and practically because when you remind yourself physically and practically then it gets deep down. Because remember, it takes

21 days to form a habit. We are not even doing this challenge for 21 days. We are doing this challenge for 10. And for some of you, these 10 days, of this 10-day challenge has been hard. In fact, you probably ready to quit after day 2 and now we are on Day 6 you can do this.

Just know it is getting ready to get hotter in here. Because I promise you, I am listening to God on what to do. We have got to make the vow and we have got to operate in the vow. And we have got to be who God has called us to be in this time because all of us are getting ready to go through transition and I am loving it. I am loving that we are going through transition, that we are stepping forward and doing things that we have been called to do, that we are being strong, that we have been appointed for just such a time as this.

Day 7 Expectation

Day #7. Can you believe it? It's so amazing to be here. And I know we have been challenged, we've been pushing it, we've been doing some things, we've been going some places, and I know that you are just as excited as I am about this challenge.

Remember, we open with the Prayer of Jabez no matter what.

"Jabez cried out to the God of Israel, 'Oh, that you would bless me and enlarge my territory! Let your hand be with me, and keep me from harm so that I will be free from pain.' And God granted his request."

All right now, now is the time. Remember, that we must make it personal and make it intentional.

"Deborah cried out to the God of Israel, "Oh, that you would bless me and enlarge my coaching business, my publishing business, increased platforms to speak on, and to be an international – have more international dates. Let your

---

hand be with me and keep me from harm so that I will be free from everyone that has misused me, everybody that has handled me wrong, church hurt, anybody that has – that I've been – that has used verbal abuse to take control of me.' And God granted me my request."

All right, guys. I'm going to give you a second and if you notice, my making it personal and making it intentional has kind of changed over the course of the past 7 days, which is fine because when you are making this personal and intentional, it might change. You may have to add some things. You may take some things out, because soon God is going to start to reveal some more things to you that are holding you back from your territory being enlarged.

Now, let us take it to the next step. You already know we have our word for the day. Our word for today is expectation. OK, let us just go with the definition because I'm so excited about expectation.

Expectation is a noun, a strong belief that something will happen or be the case in the future. Expectation.

So, you are praying this prayer. You have faith. You have increased your faith. You have written your vow. Now, it is time for you to have the belief that it is going to happen. And when you have a strong expectation, that means you believe that it's going to happen and that it is going to happen in the future, that it is something that's going to be revealed to you. You are going to do it and whatever you are praying for, you are believing God to do it because that is where your faith is being activated.

Now, the works, remember faith without works is what? Dead! So even though you are expecting it to happen, you must be doing the work so when it does happen, you are ready to walk into it. So, it goes back into that whole David situation that we've been talking about is that in order for him to go from the field to the palace, before he even killed the Goliath, he was already slaying lions, tigers, and bears. So, he has already perfected his aim. He had already perfected his skill. He had already perfected what he could do.

So, while you are out here preaching and teaching to other people, you are already preparing yourself, you are already perfecting your skill, you are perfecting your voice, you are perfecting who you are. So, when that next level comes or when that that Goliath comes, you are already prepared to kill him, slay him, and knock him out so then you are ready to go on into the palace.

But if you never know or have any clear expectations, what are you working on? So, what are you expecting? What are you expecting?

You must know what you are expecting from God. You can pray this Prayer of Jabez all day long, "Enlarge my territory. Let me have this. Let me have that." But until you know for certain what that is and what you are expecting and making it clear and making it plain, even though you put a few things in that prayer but how do you want it to manifest itself? How do you want to see your territory enlarged? Or what are you expecting to happen when your territory does enlarge? Because that's what you need to be thinking. What are you expecting?

Because God is getting ready to take you to the platforms that you want. He is getting ready to put you in front of the people that you want. But you got to be able to answer the questions. If you are ready to open your business or you have done the business plan, you've been actually saying you want a cleaning business. You've been out here talking about, "I'll clean your house for $10. I will do this for $20." Because at the end of the day, what you have been doing is that you have been practicing on how to be more efficient in your cleaning service.

You have been getting funds in order to start to buy the equipment that you need. So, you never know whose house you go to you are charging them $50 or $60. You do such a good job. You did not know that that particular client has buildings and schools or other places that need to be cleaned and they asked you, "Can you clean this building for me?" Your territory just enlarged, guys. Your territory just enlarged but are you ready?

Are you going to sit there and said, "Oh my gosh! I have never cleaned a building." You better be ready to say, "Yeah, I got this!" I'm ready to jump through this hoop. I'm ready to figure this out because at the end of the day, you already know how to be efficient. You have already bought supplies enough in order to clean a few houses. You know right now how many bottles of bleach it takes to clean the two houses. So if you already know what it takes to clean two houses then it shouldn't be so hard for you to be ready to prepare yourself to go into battle of a big building or a nursery school, whatever it is because you've already been preparing it and you are expecting it to enlarge.

Now, what is really going to happen when enlargement happens faster than you are expecting it to, you could let the fear of success jump in and mess you up. But you cannot let expansion mess you up because then you are going to fall into that lane of doubt. You are going to fall in that lane of fear. We have talked about that. We will not let fear or things happening fast, quickly mess us up or discouraged us. You hear that word again. We talked about discouragement. We have talked about fear. We have talked about faith.

Now, we are talking about increasing your expectation because God did not put you here to be mediocre and mundane. How can you be the lender and not the borrower if you are not expecting for a larger harvest? You are not expecting for larger increase. You are not expecting for things to start moving. You are not expecting to have more than one more client. You are not expecting to have more than one building. You are not expecting to have a franchise. You are not expecting to be speaking on multiple continents within one month.

You are not expecting to have your phone ringing so much that you have to make sure that you have not one assistant but two assistants, one just to have your email and one just to answer your calls. You are not expecting to have to have multiple calendars or must start hiring a staff. You are not expecting to walk out and be able to just say, "I don't even have to look at the receipt because it's going to be paid for."

Stop living in that lane of lack. Stop living in that lane of self-doubt. Stop living in that lane of low expectations because guys, we got to be ready. It is now time. It is Day 7, which is the number of completions. You should be ready right now. That's why this falls like really well on Day 7 because when you are expecting something, that's just like a woman that is pregnant. When you know that you have something growing within you, you are expecting to give birth at the end of the nine months.

What are you expecting to birth at the end of this Prayer of Jabez Challenge? What are you expecting to birth when we get to the end and what time schedule your assigning to yourself?

And at the end of the day, we can even say, what are you expecting to have happened by the end of the year? What are you expecting in the next 6 months? What are you expecting in the next 90 days? Heck, what are you expecting to happen in this decade?

I'm just going to let you marinate on that for a little bit. I need you to really think about that, about your expectations and where you want to go and what you want to do. Because when you start to really think about what you are expecting, God is getting ready to blow your mind.

Now, I guess you will say, "What do you expect? You got us over here expecting." This is what I'm expecting. Increase in my coaching clients. Book more paid speaking opportunities. You see where I say, book more paid speaking opportunities? Because you can get a lot of speaking opportunities as a speaker, but you got to be expecting to get more paid ones. Launch my publishing company with five author clients. Yeah, that's what I'm talking about. I want to launch my business with five author clients. That is my goal. And someone will say, "Well, that's not a big goal." It is, because I'm brand new, and I want an obtainable and measurable goal. Now, if I get 10, yeah, I will be turning cartwheels, but for now, I'm expecting 5 so we can launch appropriately."

And then I want to increase my personal finances by 20%. Not what the business makes, I want to be able to pay myself 20% more than my paycheck that I receive. From all of my opportunities, I want to be able to have a profit of where my personal finances will increase by 20%, not what's in savings, not what's going back into the business, but my personal finances, what I can pay myself.

The Prayer of Jabez In the Market Place

Ya'll, that is a big goal. That means I got to hustle and run. And that means my faith and my works have got to line up with the will of God because I am expecting big things for this year. I am not even putting that on the decade because these are things that I should be able to accomplish – no, that I will accomplish within a year.

What are you putting on your goals? Which leads us to your favorite part of everything that we have done throughout this challenge, your homework, develop your expectations list. Yeah, I am real serious about that. Develop your expectations list. Pray that God will reveal to you how to accomplish your expectations. Again, faith without works is dead.

Then post your expectations. Your expectations that you have are going to be specific and intentional, and that's what you're going to be praying for because you should resemble what you already put in your Prayer of Jabez of how you want your territory to be enlarged and are digging a little deeper into where you're going.

I want you to post your expectations because you can do this. You have the power within you to do it and it will be done. You have got to get ready for this because I know I am ready. I know this challenge has been a challenge for me as

The Prayer of Jabez In the Market Place

well. Do not think that I'm giving you stuff that I'm not doing myself. Do not think that I'm not being challenged and pushed just like you are because I am, because I'm doing the work right with you.

God is revealing something new, something different to do. And that is what you want to see in your prayer life. That is what you want to see in your expectations. That's what you want to see when your territory enlarges, because it can enlarge one way and then God would have you go back and do some of the things and then you see it enlarge in a different way.

I cannot wait to come back and tell you all some of the things of how God has been enlarging because of the work that I have been putting in. Every time God takes me to another level, I must go back and for lack of better statement, reevaluate what I've done.

And so, that means that I can save money by doing things a different way. That is OK. And ladies and gentlemen, please do not feel like because you've had to regroup, because you've had to postpone that it is a sign of failure, because it is not. It is a sign of wisdom because you had the wisdom to know that instead of me going completely, for lack of better

---

statement, completely broke, you are able to pull the reins in to reevaluate what you are doing.

So now, you can come back with even more and even better and reach a larger territory. I'm ready and I'm excited for what you are going to do. I'm excited for where you are going. I'm excited for who you are going to reach. I'm excited your life being changed and the lives that you changed because your life is changing. Because you have got to enter into this with such a spirit of expectation like you never before, because when you expect God to move, I'm going to promise you, He is not going to move the way you want Him to move. He is not going to move when you think He is going to move. But when He does move, it is going to blow your mind. So baby, get ready because I cannot wait to hear your testimonies about what He is doing.

All right, guys. I know you have got a lot of work to do. I know you are probably still writing your prayers. I know you are still trying to get your vows together. But today, get to it, honey. You got to do your homework. You have got to. You have got to do what you have to do in lining up your expectations.

_____

The Prayer of Jabez In the Market Place

Oh, and another thing. When you are doing your expectations, don't overthink them. Do it almost like a brainstorming session, what pops into your mind first; write that down. Do not overthink it because when you start to overthink things then you tend to mess up.

Now, if something drops into your spirit, the first thing is, "Woohoo! That is too big. That is too much. I can't do that." That is the main thing you need to write down. Because remember, God is not going to give you something bigger than what he cannot provide for you. Because vision without provision cannot happen. God is not the author of confusion, so God is going to give you the desires of your heart, but He is also going to give you things that are going to push you to where He wants you to go.

Because remember, we are talking about walking in destiny and in purpose. And your destiny and purpose are always bigger than what you can see. And it also activates your faith because remember, faith is the substance of things hoped for and evidence of things not seen because that is what the Bible tells us.

Especially my people that are in ministry, my ministry leaders, my ministry workers. the Bible says, "Your gift will make room for you." Your gift will make room for you. You are using your gift in the marketplace, so do not be afraid to charge people what you are worth. Your gift has value.

I do not even know why I am saying this. Bu, I do know why I am saying this because that goes with you developing your expectations. And if you are expecting God to move in a mighty way then that means He is going to put the people in your path that are going to be able to afford what you are offering. They are going to be able to afford your products and services.

And again, I'm not telling you that I don't have a problem with it because I do. Until I had a coach that made me realize my worth and I should not be discouraged or lowering the worth of my goods and services.

When I started to do different things, I always price myself a lot lower than what I should have. And I am sharing this with you because I know somebody is going through this right now. You are afraid to charge $20 for your book. But when you think about what you had to put in that book, it costs you probably $60 to produce overall. But you are afraid to charge $20 because you are thinking, "Oh, nobody is going buy it."

But you know what? Somebody will. And at the end of the day, when you put your price, people pay for what they want. And people pay for things that they feel have value. And you have got to evaluate your value for yourself. When you know you have value, that even changes your expectations. I expect certain things because I know my value. I expect to be treated a certain way because I know my value. I expect to be able to do certain things because I know my value.

And when you know your value, people will start to treat you like that. And you wonder why people treat you the way they treat you is because you do not show them that you have value. And you do not show them that things that they're joking about that you value, and I know you got that. I do not have to explain it. I do not have to say anything about that. I do not have to go any further. But when you know your value, your expectations are going to become clearer and clearer and clearer.

Day 8 Image

Day 8. Can you believe it? I know we have been doing some things. We have been talking about making it personal, making it intentional. We have been talking about how we are going to get over the pain that people have caused us. We are getting ready to walk in our divine calling in what we are doing.

And so many times because we have not been intentional and/or made our prayers personal, some of these things we might think that we already have in place but, we still do not have it.

So, let us go ahead. Jump right in. You all know the routine. All right. Let us go ahead and pray the Prayer of Jabez 1 Chronicles 4:9-10.

"And Jabez cried out to the God of Israel, 'Oh, that you would bless me and enlarge my territory! Let your hand be with me and keep me from harm so that I will be free from pain.' And God granted him his request."

The Prayer of Jabez In the Market Place

All right you all, that is the Prayer of Jabez. You all know how we do it. So, let's go ahead and make it personal and make it intentional.

Deborah Franklin cried out to the God of Israel, "Oh that you would bless me and enlarge my coaching business, my speaking business that my – that I will start having more paid stages and international engagements. Let your hand be with me, and keep me from harm so that I will be free from my past hurt, people talking about me, stabbing me in the back, all the verbal abuse that I had to endure " And God granted me my request.

We made it personal. We made it intentional. So now, you know we are getting ready to do our next step, our word of the day, Image. I know you are thinking, "Why are we talking about image and we are talking about the prayer of Jabez?" When God gave this to me, He knocked my socks off.

Image is a noun, a visual representation of something. So now that you want God to enlarge your territory, now that you want God to show you your next move, what do you look like?

What do you look like? Have you looked in the mirror and decided about what you look like? What is the image that you are seeing? What is the image that you are portraying that God is showing you? What is that image?

Because when you start to think about that image, when you first look in the mirror, who do you see? Do you see that person that is broken? Do you see that person that has no hope? That has no vision.

We have been going through this Prayer of Jabez and making it personal, making it intentional, and right now, when you look in the mirror, you may not be seeing what you are anticipating. So, at that first glance, I want you to look in the mirror and that's your first glance. What do you see?

When I looked in the mirror I saw, Wonder Woman. Yes, I know that I am a Wonder Woman because once I learn balance, I am going to be able to jump into action of everything that I need to do. I will be able to do what I need to do. I am going to have the tools in my hand, in my mind, at my disposal to go ahead and conquer what I'm setting out to do. Therefore, these images work for me.

The image is who do you see or what you want to see? Because, some of you probably aren't there yet and you never even thought about putting this as part of your journey during this Prayer of Jabez because when we start looking at this whole Prayer of Jabez, we talked about enlarging our territory. We talked about all these things but who do you see when that territory is enlarged?

Who do you see when it is time to make that step? Who do you see? Are you timid? Are you not able to speak up for yourself? Are you not able to make those connections or are you still waddling in that pain that is holding you back from being who you have been called to be to walk in this season of territory enlarging?

Because at the end of the day, when you start to pray and ask God to enlarge your territory and it begins to start getting larger and larger, you are going to have to be able to balance what has happened. So, you are going to have to know how to do self-care. You are going to have to know how to say **no**. Yes, **no** must become part of that. You are going to have to know how to work on your schedule. You are going to have to know how to quiet those things, those inner things that have been slowing you down.

So in other words, you are going to have to go back and be able to quiet those things that caused you pain because usually what caused us pain are usually what happens are those hurdles that we have to go through or those obstacles that are in our way.

Yeah, think about that. And that's why we had to identify what that pain is or what that pain was because even with Jabez, Jabez had to deal with the point that his name meant pain because his mother reminded him of that she said, "I named him that because he caused me so much pain."

So how do you think that made him feel? Every day I'm reminded that I caused pain? And that is why that makes so much sense in that prayer when he says, "So I may not cause pain." So in other words, hurt people hurt people. And while we are getting our territories enlarged, if we have not dealt with that pain, we are going to see ourselves inflicting what someone has inflicted on us without even knowing it.

So while we are working, we have to start developing our image of who we want to be because once we know who we want to be and how we want to obtain it and then we get the visual of who we want to be.

You are going to have to do a mirror test. When you are thinking about what you are going through, you are going to have to look at who you are closely and then be honest with yourself.

The Prayer of Jabez In the Market Place

Now after you do this Day 8, you may have to go back to Day 1 and redo or adjust some things because it's just not what you thought it was going to be. When you were looking at one thing, you have been praying your prayers, you've been praying your vow, you've been praying your promise, you've been praying of being set free from the pain. Remember, we are praying for clarity. We are praying for change. We are praying for expansion as well. God maybe changing some things in you just because of what you are praying.

And when you look at that image, God could show you something right then about who you are for real when you look at yourself of who you really are and what you really are doing. Yes, I know. I know. Because when I did this, this was hard for me. This was extremely hard for me because I had to be honest with myself. It is not something that I could depend on someone else to tell me. I had to be honest with myself and start digging deep in who I was and what I was doing. So, you must start to think about who you are and what you are doing.

Homework. I want you to look in the mirror. Write down what you see immediately. Whatever you see, write it down. So, in other words, when you go into the mirror, you need to have that pen and paper ready for you to take notes. You are going to have to be ready to do that.

Then once you look in the mirror, you need to do it one time. The second time you need to look in the mirror again. Write down what you want to see. What changes do you need to make? And I am not talking about physical changes. That is not what I am talking about, so don't sit up here and start talking about, "Oh, I need a nose job. My lips too big. I am too dark. My eyes are not bright enough." What image do you want to see?

Remember, I have Wonder Woman and then I had a woman juggling. And that juggling means that I was putting everything in perspective because if I'm not juggling, let's say, like I'm out of order. But remember, a juggler must be on rhythm. And once that rhythm is off then things start to fall apart.

Next step draw a picture or find pictures like I can't draw, or find pictures of who you want to see in that mirror. Who do I want to see? I want to see a woman that got it together. I want to see a woman that is Wonder Woman, that has all the tools that I need to make it to the next step. I want to be that woman that when you ask a question, I am ready to go. I am ready to jump. I am ready to go. I am ready to go. I am ready to go.

Because if you think about back when we were kids and we saw Wonder Woman, she was able to jump into action and do what she had to do regardless of the situation. Even when they put her in the Justice League, she was still running things because she had things under control.

So yes, I promise you, that is what you are going to be doing. I want you to really, really, really look hard at these pictures that you choose because these are images that you are going to post. Remember, we are really big during this time of this Prayer of Jabez and God enlarging your territory that we are really big on posting remember, Habakkuk 2:2, "Write a vision, make it plain, and then share it with the heralds."

But right now, you need to write your vision, make it plain, post it so you can meditate on it day and night because that is in the Bible as well. So, we must make sure that we are doing this and being consistent with it.

I'm excited about what we are doing, where we are going, and how we are going to handle this and that God is really getting ready to do some things for you and make sure you are doing the homework. Make sure you are applying it. I just want to encourage you that this is your step into moving to where you need to be, the step to take you to that next level and know. The struggle is real. Because when I was going through an extremely dark situation, I did not know what I wanted to do. I did not know how I was going to do it. I did not know anything.

And I really did not have anybody to go to. And I keep saying, I want to go into business for myself. I want to be a speaker. I wanted to be a coach. I want to do workshops and things of that nature.

I kept asking questions and I start trying to better myself. And then I had to start to visualize who I wanted to be and how I wanted to accomplish certain things. I started putting myself in positions and making sure that I was talking to people that were doing some of the same things I wanted to do.

So again, you see how visualization helps you develop that next step. Is it easy? No, indeed. Can it be done? Yes, indeed. I know I have been pushing you, pushing you, pushing you, pushing you, and probably making you think of some things that you never had thought about before. But that is OK.

The Prayer of Jabez In the Market Place

Day 9 Armor

It's Day 9. I am excited and I know you are too because we have made it this far making The Prayer of Jabez intentional and personal, purposeful, expecting God to move and enlarge our territory. Whatever that territory looks like for you. Remember, it is going to look different for all of us. We are expecting God to do it and it is going to happen in this season.

Now, we are going to go ahead and get started with our Prayer of Jabez.

"Jabez cried out to the God of Israel, 'Oh, that you would bless me and enlarge my territory! Let your hand be with me and keep me from harm so that I will be free from pain.' And God granted his request."

All right, guys. Now, it's time for you to pray your personal and intentional prayer.

Now, this is mine.

"Deborah cried out to the God of Israel, 'Oh, that you would bless and enlarge my coaching business, my publishing company, my being on international stages for preaching and teaching. Let your hand be with me, and keep me from harm so that I will be free from people that have lied on me, talked about me, stabbed me in the back, made me a victim of verbal abuse.' And God granted me my request."

Now, you all, let us get ready for our word today is armor! You got to put on your whole armor. And you already know that the armor is a noun. It is a defensive covering for the body especially covering as a metal used in combat, a quality or a circumstance that affords protection.

The armor of prosperity, a protective outer layer as they shoot a plant, or animal or a cable, you know the little plastic that's on those things that protects the things that are natural that can go get destroyed.

We are talking about putting on the whole armor of God. Some of you need to know that you are going to have to start making sure that you have that whole armor. And that is found is Ephesians 6:10-18 NIV.

"Finally, be strong in the Lord and in His mighty power. Put on the full armor of God so that you can take your stand against the devil's schemes. For our struggle is not against the flesh and blood but against the rulers, against authorities, against powers of this darkness world, and against the spiritual forces of evil in the heavenly realm. Therefore, put on the full armor of God so that when the day of evil comes, you may be able to stand your ground and after you have done everything to stand. Stand firm then with the belt of truth, the buckle around your waist with the breastplate of righteousness in place, and with your feet fitted with the readiness that comes from the gospel of peace. In addition to all of this, take up the shield of faith with which you can extinguish all the flaming arrows of the evil one. Take the helmet of salvation and the sword of spirit which is the word of God and pray in the spirit on all occasions, all kinds of prayers and requests. With this in mind, be alert, and always keep on praying for all the Lord's people."

So not only do you have to put on the full armor, you must pray and pray in the spirit, pray in your heavenly language. And not only pray for yourself but pray for others.

You are already prepared for this. You just must recognize that you already have the armor on you. You already have the armor with you. You already have that breastplate of

---

righteousness. You already have that buckle around your waist and that you are ready to go into war.

But some of you have forgotten that you already have what you need to go out in war and be able to fight the battle and win. Some of you are feeling like you can't win but I tell you today, we declare and decree today that you have the power and you are able to accomplish everything that you have set out to do.

You are called for this season. You are called to walk in the area that you want to walk in. You are called to stand up and be strong and know that God is getting ready to enlarge your territory like never before.

God is getting ready to blow your mind. God is getting ready to take you to levels that you never thought you would make. God is getting ready to open doors for you that you never thought would open. God is getting ready to show you like never before that everything that you had to go through was for you to have a testimony to be able to conquer what you set out to do.

Let's look at David. David was the youngest brother of all of them. David was the one that nobody thought could do anything. David was the one that was in the field. He was always in the field. He was killing lion, tigers, and bears. He was doing everything that he was supposed to do. But that was preparing him for his Goliath.

Now, you have been in this field. You have gone to school. You got the degree. You have had the job. You have been through the failed relationships. Now, you have been to all of these training sessions. You have been through this, all these coaches. You have done everything that you know to do to get to where you needed to be. But you have been wondering, "Why have I not gotten there?" What is setting me back? What is taking me off my kilter? What is hindering me?

You have forgotten that you have the whole armor of God. That this is war time. You have forgotten it is time to go to war. And in order to go to war, your armor can't look like someone else's.

I'm going to let you sit there and marinate on that. Your armor cannot look like someone else's. Let's think about David and King Saul and I'm going to call it the David and King Saul Rule. David was getting ready to go fight Goliath. He had told them, "I can do this."

Saul said, "Here is my armor. Wear my armor into battle." David said, "This armor is too big for me. It's too heavy for me. This armor was not designed for me in mind. This armor was not created for me to go into war."

Yes, you have gone to school. Yes, you have got the coaches. Yes, you have been through the seminars. Yes, you got all the certificates. But you have got to take what you need and transform it into who you are, because when you go into war you have to know what you are fighting with and what you are fighting for. You are fighting for you. You are fighting for your family, your husband, your wife, your children, your inheritance, your legacy.

And if you are fighting for you, you cannot go out looking like somebody else. Yeah, you could imitate people for so long but at the end of the day, you have got to know who you are. You have got to become authentically you. That is why you must make this Prayer of Jabez personal and intentional because when it's personal and intentional, you must grab hold to it a little tighter.

It is just like when you have somebody else's towel, it is different when it's yours and when it's somebody else's. It is different when it is your job and instead of somebody else's. It is different when it is your church and somebody else's. It is different when you have prepared the lesson and your delivery. Know that you are ready.

You are ready for this war. And all you are going to need is the slingshot that was designed for you, the stones that were designed for you and most of all, you are wearing the armor designed for you.

When you are getting ready to go into war, know that you are going in the name of the Father, the Son, and the Holy Ghost. You are getting ready to take that everywhere you go. I do not care if you are going into the classroom. I do not care if you are going into the boardroom. I do not care if you are getting ready on stage to preach to millions of people. I do not care if you are going on the stage to speak to thousands of people. I don't care if you are going in a conference room to share your brand-new idea. But God has prepared you for this. God has set you up for this. And now, it's up to you to walk down to the battlefield. And know that you are ready.

Now, I'm not going to tell you this is not going to be easy every day. I'm not going to tell you that you are not going to have obstacles. I'm not going to tell you that you are not going to have distractions. But know that you are ready for this battle, that you are getting ready to walk out and most of

---

The Prayer of Jabez In the Market Place

all, you know you are going to win because all that other stuff that you went through was setting you up for this. It was a setup to get you right here, a setup, because it's time to go to war.

Yeah, it's time to go to war. We are ready. We are ready. Yes, we are!

Homework. What does your armor look like? Now, I'm going to break it down like this. Some of you, your armor is going to look like social media. Your armor is going to look like doing classes online. Your armor is going to look like writing books. Your armor is going to look like developing speeches to go out and share with people. Some of you, your armor is going to look like showing somebody how they can take something, their simple business and making it something more.

For me, my armor is going to look like showing educators how they can take what they know and turn into a different stream of income. I know that my armor is going to look like being a publisher for women in ministry that want to get their word out and want to be with the publisher they can trust with their word and trust with their vision. I know what my armor is going to look like. What does your armor look like?

What will be your strategy to win? Does that mean that you need to find someone to coach you? Does that mean that you need to ask for help? For some, the biggest strategy is asking somebody for help. Does that mean that you got to start being honest with yourself and being intentional with yourself on what you want to do and what you want to accomplish? And to start to purpose in your life and purpose out of your mouth, purpose in your thoughts, because I declare and decree that it shall be done. I declare and decree that this war, you will win, and you will win big.

God is getting ready to do it for you. The question is, are you ready? And you know what? At the end of the day, it does not matter if you are ready or not because whatever God has destined you to do, you will do it. You will do it. You will do it however you got to do it because you are destined to win. You are destined to succeed because you would not be going through this challenge if you were not ready for your territory to enlarge. Yes, indeed.

Day 10 Winning

Day 10. Woohoo! We made it. We made it. We made it. We made it. We made it. Yes, we have made it to Day 10 of the Prayer of Jabez Challenge. I am excited. I do not even know what to tell you. I am so excited about us reaching to Day 10 because I will be honest with you, getting to this point has been a challenge for me. It has been a challenge because I didn't realize how much stuff I had going on at one time. It was like I knew I had plan to do this, I knew that I was going to be reaching out, I knew I wanted to do another challenge at the beginning of the year, I knew I wanted to change the format, but I was like, "God, really?"

And so, it has been a challenge because I knew God was taking me somewhere and I knew that I had been praying that God would enlarge my territory. But honestly, I did not think it was going to happen this fast, this quick, and the way that it is going because it has really been blowing my mind. And I am hoping that you have the same testimony of how things have started to blow your mind.

I've had friends that have called me for certain things and I just answered immediately and then the next day, I see somebody else that's totally not connected to us saying the same thing and it's like, "Oh my God! That's confirmation" When God is speaking the same thing, it's just like when we start to hear all the prophets begin to say that they felt like there was a shifting in the atmosphere and things were about to change and we needed to get ready. And those who were last were now getting ready to be first. Those that did not have a name, now people are going to be calling their name and recognizing their name.

Yes, we are being intentional, and we are making it personal and it is Day 10. I am so happy and proud to say it. I'm so excited about where we are going.

Now, let's go ahead and pray our Prayer of Jabez.

"And Jabez cried out to the God of Israel, 'Oh, that you would bless me and enlarge my territory. Let your hand be with me, keep me from harm so that I will be free from pain.' And God granted his request."

Make it personal and intentional, here is mine.

"Deborah cried out to the God of Israel, 'Oh, that you would bless me and enlarge my coaching business, my publishing company, my speaking on platforms on national and international stages. Let your hand be with me, and keep me from harm so I that I will be free from the pain of verbal abuse, people stabbing me in the back, regret.' And God granted me my request."

Whoa! Yeah! I feel free already. How many of you are feeling free? Feeling free. All right, you know what's next. Our word of the day is winning! We are winning! Winning! Winning! Yes, I'm excited about winning.

It is an adjective, gaining, resulting in, relating to victory in a contest or competition. But you know what? We are talking about gaining and resulting in, relating to victory in what we are doing. We are not in a contest. We are not in a competition. Well, in a way, we are because we are competing to be first in everything that we do. We want to be first in our businesses. We want to be first in our ministries. We want to be first because we know God is getting ready to use us like never before. So, we are winning. We are winning because we finished this 10-day challenge. We are winning because we have identified our pain and God is going to release that from us.

We are winning because we have made our vows. We are winning because we have set things in motion of where we want God to enlarge our territory. We are winning because we have set aside the time to identify who we are and whose we are and what we want to accomplish. We are winning because we have taken the steps to move in the direction that we know God has called us to do. We are winning because we are God's ordained and anointed ones for this time, this season, for what we are doing. We are winning!

I do not even know how you are able to sit still because I feel like running right now. I just feel the mighty move of God in this place, in this situation, and God is going to do it right now. I tell you right now, whatever God tells you to do, you have got to do it. Wherever God tells you to go, you have got to go because in this season, it is no holds barred. And do not ask for anything if you are not expecting it to be done. So be careful about what you let come from your mouth because it will be manifested. You cannot come into this situation, come into this season with doubt or hurt or feeling of lack. You have got to always feel like you are winning.

Keep pushing! Keep pushing! Keep pushing! Keep pushing because we got to push. We got to push. We got to push. We got to push. We got to push because now, we got to make it to that finish line because we have got to show people that because we are saved, because we have been ordained, because we have been called to ministry that we are winning. And we can look like what we want to look like and not what we have been through.

We got to win! And we got to win in every area of our life! We also have to make sure we are taking care of ourselves-self-care. Remember that it's OK to make mistakes. It's OK to have bad days. It's OK to be less than perfect. It's OK to do what's best for you, to be yourself. **It's OK.**

And don't let anybody tell you that it isn't. Don't let anybody tell you that you can't take an hour to yourself, that you can't take a personal retreat for a couple of days. And I know some of you are saying right now, "Well, I don't have the money for that." Find it. Find it. You can use Groupon. You can Priceline. You can do a lot of things that will give you discounted rates. Get up and go!

And then maybe if you really are in that situation, go to the park. It's free. Find somebody that may even have a friend that has a pool, tell them that you will come sit there for a while. So, you can commune with yourself and God, your creator. Because sometimes we can be so tired and feeling empty that we just need God to download some things in us. That we just need to walk around and just listen. And how about this, if you do not hear anything, be OK with not hearing anything.

In this time of our winning, your biggest win is going to be to yourself. When you learn to take care of you and value you, you are going to be winning like never before. Self-care, because a lot of times people are falling out when they make it because they never knew how to take a break.

Learn how to say no, because sometimes, you just sitting still is what God wants you to do because He has to make sure that you are rested and ready to go to that next competition because you are winning.

I need you to repeat after me, "It's time to get it. We will win." It is time to get it. We will win. So, whatever you are doing, whatever you are going after, you are going to get it and you are going to win.

Homework. Yes, you have homework on your last day. Your homework, homework, homework, homework, homework, yes, you got homework. You must get to work. Stay focused. Wear your armor with pride. You can only go to battle with what will fit on you.

The Prayer of Jabez In the Market Place

I know it, baby. Wear it with pride. And do not let folk or things distract you. You cannot let the people around you, or situations distract you. I do not care if it's your finances. I do not care if it's your cousin. I do not care if it is your parents, your children, your dog, your cat. I do not care what it is. Do not let it distract you from your journey, because you will reach that finish line. And for some of you, you will reach that Promised Land. Some of you you're looking at, "I want to do this because I want to buy a house. I want to get a new car. I want to get some new shoes." Whatever that thing is, start to think about that in your mind.

I hope that you have enjoyed this 10-day challenge. I hope that this 10-day challenge has done something for you. I hope that you have been able to rock with me through the course of these 10 days and that you will share this with your family, your friends, your cousins, your co-workers, whomever because it is time for us to be intentional and personal about what we are doing. And if we can just apply it to everything that we are doing because we are winning, and we are going to win. Remember, it is only lonely at the top if you don't take anybody with you.

Special Thanks

Amy Philpott

Sonya Williams Floyd

Sondra Hill-Ward

Myra Cottman

Tracy Shorter

Tiffany Durden

Sharon Taylor-White

Rosalind Jones

Lory Simmons

Talesha Jones

Ola Franklin

Mark Franklin

Justin Daniels

Norma Vigilant

Rev. Steve & Debra Taylor

Rev. Lloyd & Janelle Jones

Tracy Young

Sereta Collington

Precilla Belin

Rynette Upson

Deborah A. Franklin

Helps women in ministry and educators develop multiple streams of income by telling their story. Deborah Franklin also has a heart for women to expand their mindsets past what they can see. As a survivor of verbal abuse, she has learned to rise above what has been said to her and about her to be the authentic representative of who she is created to be.

Deborah Franklin is the author of 'adjective,' '21 Days 21 Minutes of Prayer & Meditation,' and "#5 30 Days of Motivation & Inspiration," "The Prayer of Jabez In The

---

The Prayer of Jabez In the Market Place

Marketplace," podcast host of Conversations w/Deborah Franklin and a media coach. Deborah has been working as a media coach for several years with clients who are authors, speakers and entertainers.

Deborah also uses her platform to give other aspiring artist and outlet to let their talents shine. Her ultimate goal in life is to help others to ignite the power within to propel them to their destiny while walking in their destiny.

Contact/Booking Information

Website   www.deborahfranklin.com

Email   info@deborahfranklin.com